Grandma's Carrot

A KaDe Creation

Published by Yawn Publishing LLC
2555 Marietta Hwy, Ste 103
Canton, GA 30114
www.yawnspublishing.com

Library of Congress Control Number:2021902321

ISBN:978-1-954617-03-2

Printed in the United States of America

This true story was penned by author, Karen DeSue, as it happened to her when she was quite young. The narrative is told as through her recollection and memory. She shares in hopes of providing laughter, smiles, love and lift to those who may need it. Here's hoping you enjoy reading Grandma's Carrot.

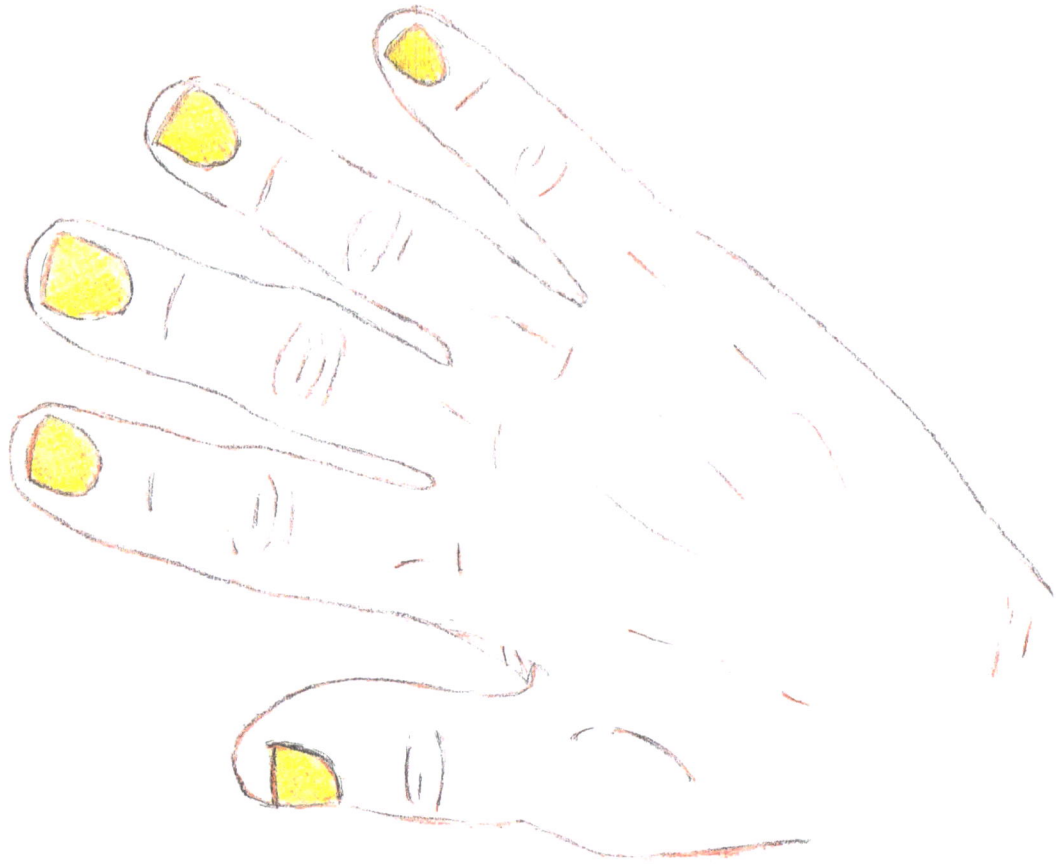

Very soon after a fifteenth birthday,
Grandpa stopped by on his way and did say,
He needed to borrow a girl for her hand,
'Twas thought the right size for his neatly laid plan.
Surprise was in store for the one 'twas his love,
For the upcoming Christmas, he hoped would be done.

He'd saved and worked diligently to design,
A fashionable piece, yes, a one-of-a-kind.
He borrowed the girl and they rode in his truck,
He worked in construction (in sawdust and muck),
They talked as he drove, he expertly explained,
The gift, the surprise, a request to be made.

It would be unique – a piece to be treasured,
The meaning and value would be beyond measure.
To represent family, their children of six,
With a stone on the top, adding him to the mix.

A circle of diamonds made into a ring,
The one on the top for a little more bling.

Surprise was the plan, so they'd keep it a secret
Until the reveal when she'd forever keep it.

Surprise!

He needed the girl for her fingers would be
The same size as Grandma's (he was guessing, you see!).
So she became part of his fun and his scheme,
They were "partners in crime", though this was his dream.

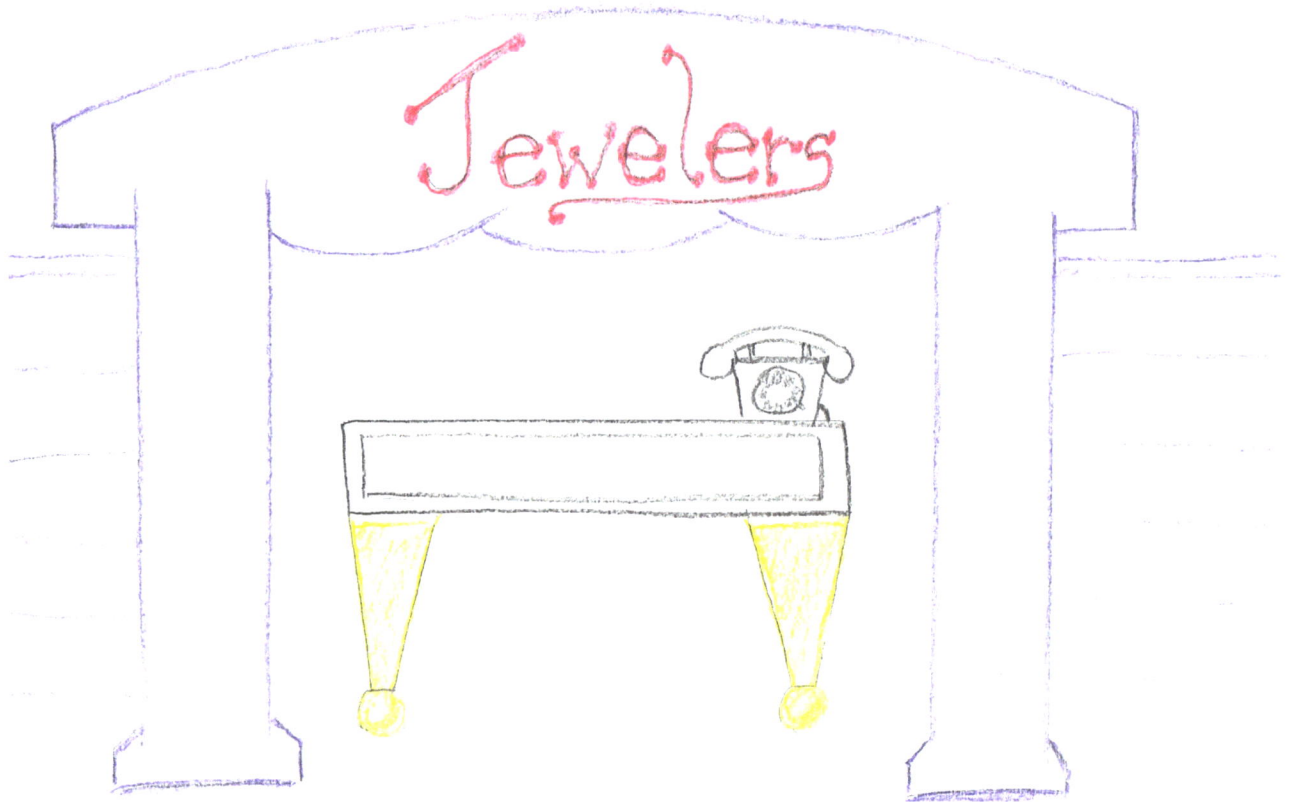

So into the jewelry store they went together,
Description was given, the girl's finger measured.
"Could its weight be a carat?" asked Grandpa with ease,
"We'll do that for you," said the jeweler quite pleased.
Work began shortly it would take some time,
A call when done promised to Grandpa was fine.
Back he would go when the job was complete,
He'd inspect, then pay for the wonder, this feat.

Time quickly passed, Grandpa picked up the ring,
He stopped by the house to ask just one more thing,
He spoke to the girl asking one more mere favor,
"Could you wrap it nicely – a way she would savor?"
"Of course!" she replied as she saw his eyes twinkle.
"Remember it's special, so add in some sprinkle!"

The mind of the young girl churned on his aim,
She knew it was secret and, boy, was she game!
She went right to work, then hooked in a twist,
She gathered supplies and became quite elfish.

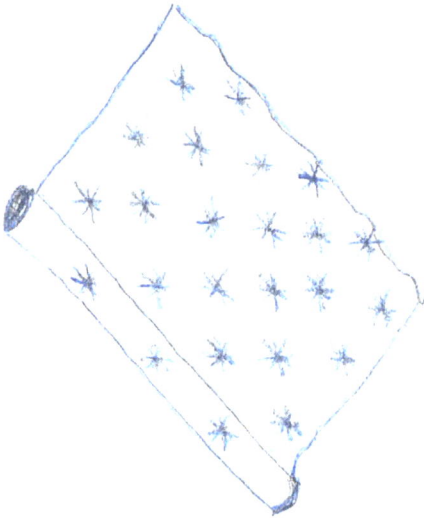

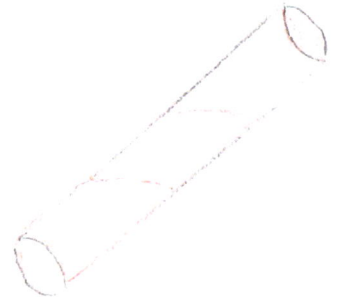

Holiday wrap, festive ribbon to twist,
And a paper towel tube 'cause she couldn't resist.
She flew to the fridge and opening the door,
She knew that she needed just one item more.

A carrot with greenery on top she did find,
Her own mother thought the girl had "lost her mind".
Wrapping the carrot in plastic would protect,
The precious commodity in this project.

A carat on a carrot would certainly render,
A beloved Christmas gift Grandma would always remember.
So wrapped in this manner the gift looked like candy,
The surprise was all set, the secret a dandy!

Then Christmas morning the phone rang quite early,
Grandpa was laughing, "She loves the gift, girlie!"

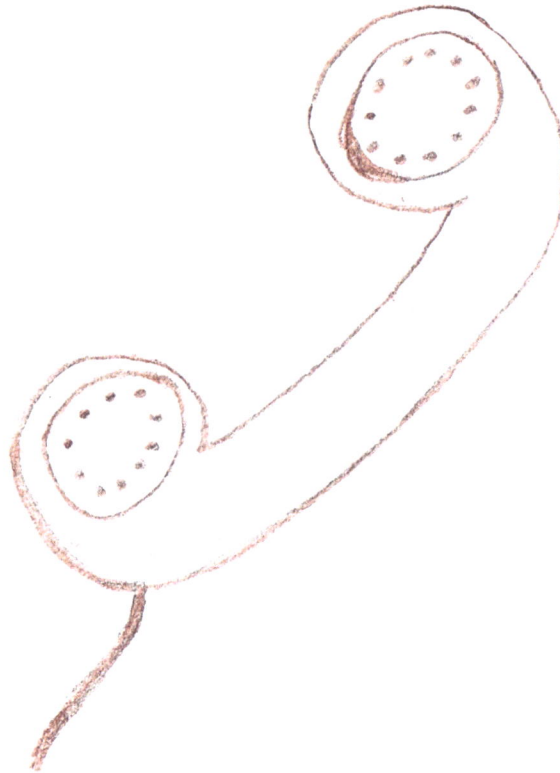

The years went by quickly, the ring often worn,
The young girl grew up, but then feelings were torn.
A call came reporting of grandfather's passing,
Grandma continued, the fond memories lasting.
Several years later, and Grandma does age,
She calls on the "girlie", then she sets the stage.

The granddaughter hears her and willingly drives,
To Grandma's to visit, she sits and complies.
After shuffling about, a small tube did appear,
Attached were remains of bygone Christmas cheer.

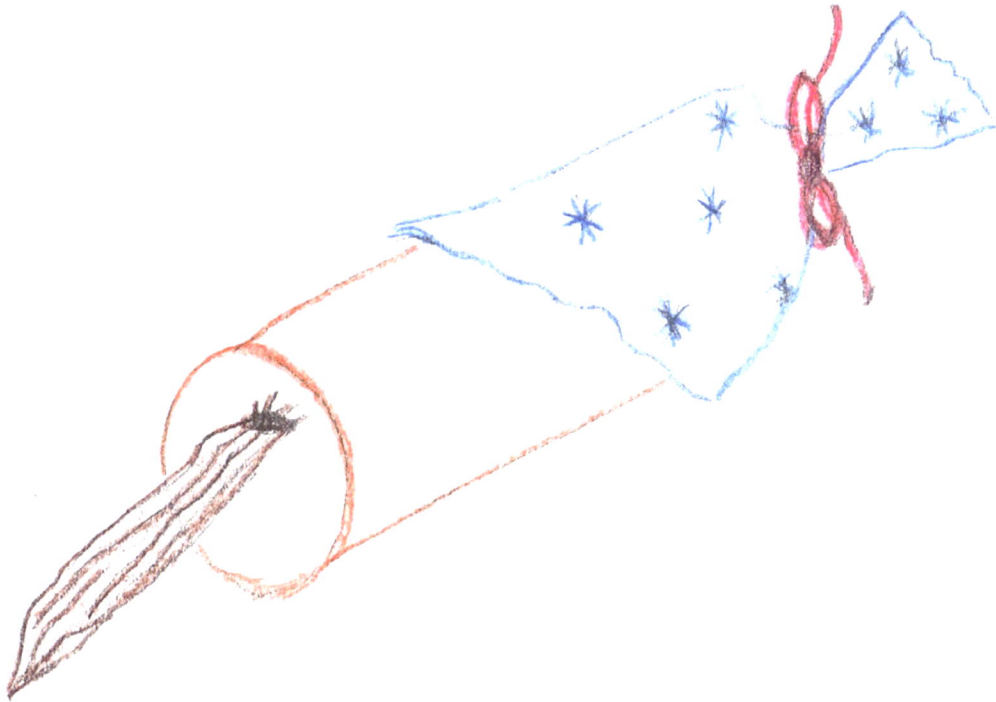

The tube coughed up a piece petrified and quite brown,
Grandmother's laughter began to abound.
"Grandma, what is this?" the young girl did parrot.
The retort came giggling, "Don't you see? It's the carrot!"

The carrot was kept three decades in a drawer,
Today was a day when the memory became more.
A box was then given, inside contained tissue,
"I want you to have this," Grandma said without issue.
The girl's eyes did mist when she unwrapped the thing,
Found inside the tissue was grandmother's ring.
The very one purchased in secret with measure,
It was a gift given the girl could now treasure.

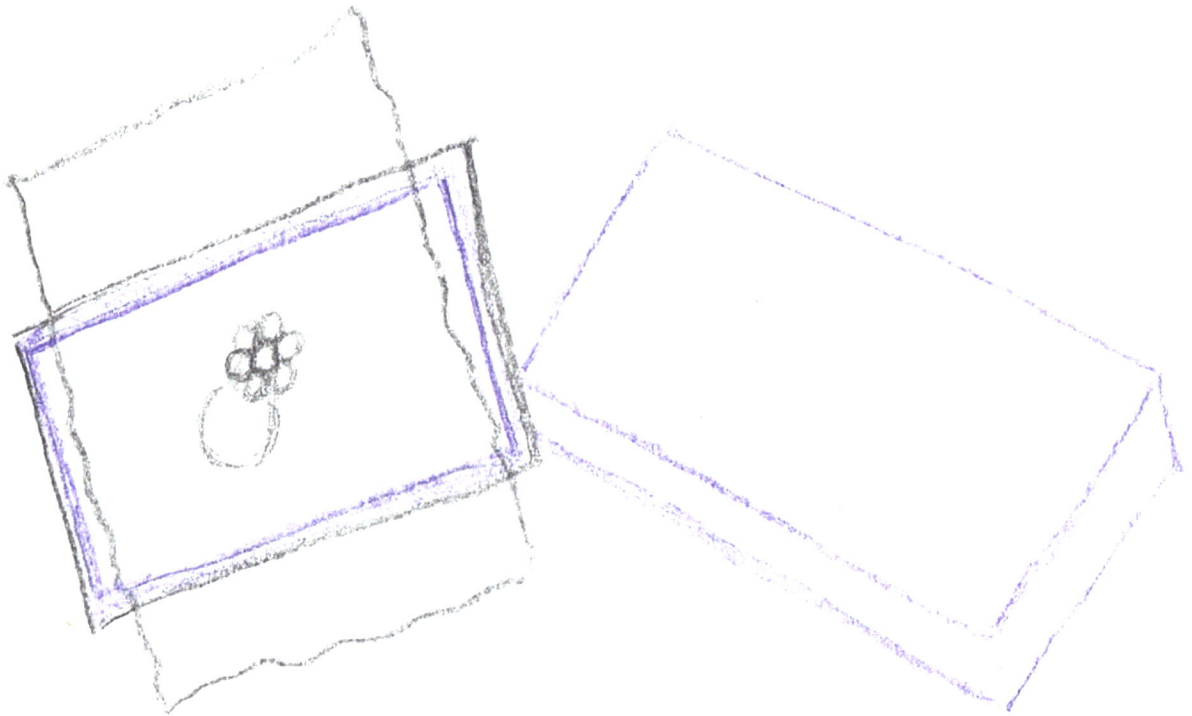

The carat on a carrot giving laughter and love,
Of family remembered both precious and beloved.
Completing the story that now has been given,
These days my Grandmother resides in Heaven.
The carat on a carrot? The story is true!
Grandpa, Grandma and me – now you know it, too!

Epilogue

Grandma's ring was purchased many years ago when Grandpa asked my mother's permission for me to accompany him to the jewelry store. My finger was used as a measure for her hand, and Grandpa "excused" me from the store so that he could "settle-up" with the jeweler. A great laugh was had over the "wrapping" of the gift on Christmas morning by both Grandma and Grandpa, who lived just down the hill from us.

Before Grandma's passing, she bequeathed the ring to me as a surprise. Its picture is found here and is treasured as a wonderful remembrance of their love for one another and their family.

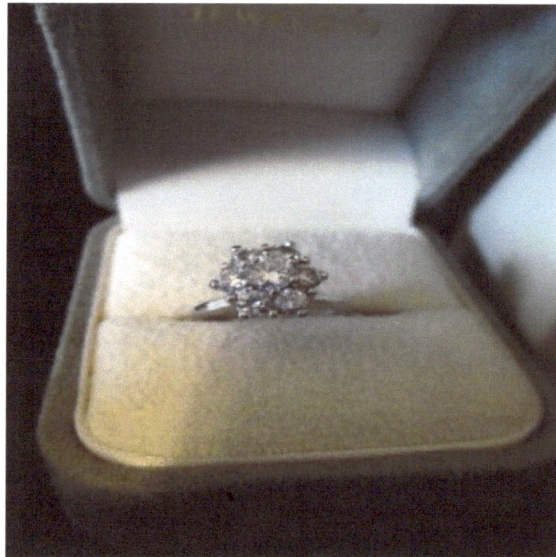

Vocabulary

(Meanings from Webster's Dictionary)

Accompany = To go with as an associate or companion. She accompanied me to the store.

Bequeath = To give or leave by will – used especially of personal property; a ring bequeathed

Carat = A unit of weight for precious stones equal to 200 milligrams

Carrot = A biennial herb with a usually orange spindle-shaped edible root

Comply = To conform, submit, or adapt as required or requested

Diligent = Characterized by steady, earnest and energetic effort; painstaking; a diligent worker.

Enlist = To secure the support and aid of; employ in advancing an interest

Petrified = Converted into stone through a slow process of mineralization; petrified wood

About KaDe

KaDe (pronounced Kay-Dee) is the pen name used by Karen DeSue, a former teacher who spent 32 years in the classroom with grades ranging from 4-12. She held students to a high standard – both academically and behaviorally, logging 19 years in Ohio and 13 years in Georgia.

She enjoys spending time with her husband and family, reading, writing, walking, and being at the beach.

www.ingramcontent.com/pod-product-compliance
Lightning Source LLC
LaVergne TN
LVHW072105070426

835508LV00003B/282